A Blue Birthday

Daniel Jacobs

Illustrated by Bill Petersen

A Harcourt Achieve Imprint

www.Rigby.com
1-800-531-5015

"Are you sure?" Mom asked.
"Do you really want blue frosting?"

Jasmine looked at the beautiful cake
they had baked.
"Please, Mom!" she said. "It's Maya's
favorite color!"

Maya was Jasmine's best friend,
and Jasmine was giving her
a surprise birthday party.
Jasmine watched as her mother
added blue food coloring
to the mixing bowl.
In seconds the frosting was the color
of the sky.
It was like magic!

After the cake was frosted, Mom laughed.
"This is the first blue cake I have ever made, but it does look good!
I'd better blow up the balloons before our guests arrive.
Will you clean up this stuff and make the sandwiches?"

"Sure, Mom!" Jasmine answered.

Jasmine took the meat, cheese, lettuce, tomatoes, and other sandwich fixings out of the refrigerator.
She made the sandwiches.
Then she filled two pitchers, one with milk and the other with water.
Mom had already made her famous potato salad.

Jasmine checked the clock.
The party would not start until 12:00.
She still had time to make more magic.
After all, if a blue cake looked good,
wouldn't more blue food be even better?

By noon all of the guests had arrived. They tried to be quiet as they waited for the birthday girl.

"Surprise!" they yelled as Maya walked through the door.

Maya looked around the room.
"Wow!" she said.
"Everything is my favorite color.
Thanks so much!"

Then Maya hugged her best friend.
"Jasmine!" said Maya.
"Only you could have thought of all this!"

Jasmine was proud. Maya was happy.
Everyone else was having fun, too.
Jasmine's big brother Bryan made
balloon animals.
He made everyone laugh.

When Mom said it was time to eat, everyone hurried into the kitchen.

"Wait until you see this!" Jasmine told Maya.

But when everyone got into the kitchen, it was Jasmine's turn to be surprised.

"OOOH!" said Maya.
It was not a happy sound.
Someone started to laugh.

Jasmine tried not to cry.
"Bryan," she whispered, "I added blue
food coloring to make the meal special.
But it's a big mess!"

"Don't worry," he whispered back.
"I know what to do."

Bryan grabbed a spoon and scooped some potato salad into his mouth.
"Mmm," he said, smiling.
"Mom, this is the best salad you've ever made!
I really like it blue!"

Next Bryan bit into a sandwich that was
dripping with blue goo.
"You know," he said, "blue food tastes
just as good as the regular kind
and it's much better looking."

Then Bryan poured some of the blue milk
into a glass.
"Who wants some?" he asked
with a smile.

"Look!" said Maya. "Look at Bryan!
I want blue teeth, too!"
She grabbed a sandwich.
Soon everyone was eating and showing off
their blue smiles.

Right before it was time for cake,
Mom pulled out her camera.
"OK!" she said, "say
'true-blue friends,' everybody!"

It was the best blue birthday ever!